love,
heartbreak
and and hangovers

shadress denise

I0134434

© 2018 Shadress Denise
© 2018 Blue Indigo Publishing, LLC

ISBN-13: 978-0-9981484-5-8
ISBN-10: 0-998141-5-8

Publisher | Blue Indigo Publishing, LLC
Book Cover Designer | ColorMeBlu Designs
www.colormebludesigns.com
Interior Design | Strawberry Publications, LLC
www.strawberrypublications.com

All rights reserved. This book contains material protected under International and Federal Copyright Laws and Treaties. Any unauthorized reprint or use of this material is prohibited. No part of this book may be reproduced or transmitted in any form or by any means, electronic or mechanical, including photocopying, recording or by any information storage and retrieval system without express writer permission from the author/publisher.

This is a work of fiction. Any references or similarities to actual events, real people, living or dead, or to the real locals are intended to give the novel a sense of reality. Any similarity in other names, characters, places, and incidents are entirely coincidental.

also written by shadress denise

poetry....
Disturbia
hello. goodbye. never again
LIBERATED
Late Night Thoughts

novels....
Who Do You Love?
Who Do You Love Too?
Smitten Kitten

coming soon....
Tales of a Recovering Love Addict
The Side Chick Chronicles

thank yous

Once again God, you cease to amaze me. Even in the peak of darkness, you find a way to be a light. When my thoughts go quiet and I can't quite find the words to write; you whisper in my ear. I will always be fascinated by you. I will always be grateful for your faith in me. I will always be in awe of your divine purpose. My gift are my words and I will continue to inspire, uplift, and share them with the world.

This book ironically came at the point I hadn't written poetry in almost five years. Disturbia was the last book of poetry I had written and for whatever reason, I hadn't written an ounce of poetry since I had finished that book. Maybe I had been cured of my broken heart, or maybe I had become so disconnected and numb, I couldn't feel anything to trigger what helped me write. I am laughing as I type this because I remember the exact moment when I was thinking to myself, *"I haven't written poetry in a long time, and I miss it."* It was almost like I had activated something within my soul and BOOM before it knew it, I finished this book. Two hundred and ninety-five poems in three months, when I had only challenged myself to write 200 poems. I vividly remember hitting the 200th poem and was feeling like *it's not finished, I have more to say.* See that's the thing with me and poetry, I always know when it's the last poem because it's like something whispers in my spirit...this is it. I always felt like it was God telling this is done and it's time to close this chapter and move on to the next great adventure. Before I knew it, I had finished this book and Late-Night Thoughts in a matter of six months. Originally, I was prepared to release this book first and then Late-Night Thoughts, but for some reason, I felt this one should be released second. With roughly 600 poems written, I was back to where it all began, and I couldn't be happier.

To all my friends and family who have supported me, thank you. Your love, and support encourages me to be better at my craft and to keep pushing forward with my dreams.

To the readers who picked up a copy of my madness, please enjoy. There are no titles and there is no order in which they fall. The love, heartbreak and occasional hangovers are scattered throughout the pages. Sometimes I feel order can be a bit chaotic. Most of the time, I feel structure can take away from the authenticity of how things should flow. Absorb the words and whatever you feel they should be called to you; write the name in the blank spaces.

Until next time, blessings & love.

shadress denise

dedication

To love... one day we won't end in heartbreak.

1: _____

I realized showing love

only got me hurt.

He could never see

who I really was,

who I wanted to be,

and there were few people

who could truly handle

my broken kind of love.

2: _____

I'm not for hurting anyone,

but I'm not for being

hurt anymore either.

Love blinds people.

Love blinded us.

It gave us room

to make excuses

for the fucked-up shit

that was in front of us

and it seems

that's all we've been doing.

Those kinds of days are over

for me and you.

3: _____

Surrender
and run away.
Run as fast as you can,
and as far as your feet
will allow you to run.
I'm no good for you.
There's nothing I can do
for your soul.
Nothing I can say
that would make you feel
this love is worth saving.
I'm no good for you,
so please stop fighting me,
stop trying to save me,
& just run away.

4: _____

Why I love him, I can't explain.

Maybe it's the simplicity

surrounding him

that brings a smile across my lips.

Though loving him

from a distance is easier

than loving him up close.

The closer he is,

the more he breathes my air,

the blinder I become.

Sometimes it's inevitable

to see clearly when

you are in love.

#5: _____

We've been artificially

programed

to believe in the fantasies of love,

and its unrealistic expectations,

rather than facing the reality

that this situation,

the one we are stuck in

right now,

has absolutely nothing

to do with love.

#6:

_____

I think we often confuse

possessiveness with love.

We label it love,

but this is not love.

Love is not a controlling emotion,

yet it has been corrupted to the point

where there is not an ounce

of purity within it.

We carry on throwing the word around

in the most cavalier way,

but I am learning to call things

for what they are

whether my feelings get hurt or not,

whether you decide to stay or leave.

Love is telling the truth

and when there is no truth,

there is no love.

#7: _____

I
think
about
him
and my
entire
soul
lights up.

#8: _____

I live and breathe life

through impulse and the right now.

I don't dwell on tomorrow

or what the future may hold.

I don't dream about

happily ever after's with him

because our love

may end before that comes.

There is no forever with me

because I may never see tomorrow.

I am content in knowing that today

I love him, and he loves me.

#9: _____

Love is bitter and its sweet.

It holds you tight

and then it releases you

without a single goodbye.

I'm not sure I want to see love

turn its back on me again.

To me, it's easier

to avoid engaging in

conversations with love.

It's simpler to avoid

touching love's hand.

I am afraid of love's

betrayal,

it's disappointment,

it's cruel, and cold shoulder.

Love without a doubt

is a bittersweet thing.

#10: _____

Tell me is it possible

to fall out of love with someone?

Or could it be

you may have never

loved them to begin with?

Can you honestly

love a person one moment

and then wake up

and not feel a thing

for them the next?

What is that called?

Where can I find

the prescription for this?

Is it boredom, love,

infatuation—

or obsession?

Could it be the emotions

I believed were there

were nothing more

than my imagination?

How I do decipher between

what I feel,

what I want you to feel,

and what I know you feel?

How do I tell myself

I don't love you any more

so I can let go?

#11: _____

I can no longer

fall in love with love.

I can no longer be love's

close, and personal confidant.

It is too painful, too sharp,

too hard to let go of

when it hurts.

Love lingers and no matter

how much time passes,

and I fight to be rid of it,

it is still buried within me.

#12: _____

Love is a

beautiful emotion.

It is even beautiful

when it has been

tarnished,

and its innocence

has been

fractured,

disintegrated,

& shattered,

into pieces we

no longer recognize.

A work of art open to a

plethora of interpretations.

#13: _____

I believe love does not show

it's true self

to me until it is lost,

until it has been given away

and no longer wanted.

I believe I do not value

love until I have

nothing to value it at all.

#14: _____

I smile at the possibility
of one day,
someone looking at me
as if nothing else matters.
Someone holding my heart
close to theirs.
Someone touching a part
of my soul
I've never wanted to share.
Someone, anyone
to come along and remind me
what it felt like to not see it
through these jaded eyes.

I want to remember love.

#15: _____

I have seen so much

I am hiding from love.

I don't know

if I can surrender again.

I don't know

if I can succumb

to that obsession anymore.

I am in love with love,

but love doesn't love me.

So, what am I to do now?

#16: _____

He talks to me in my sleep

and I listen with my soul.

I never see him,

but I know that he is here.

I know he is watching me

as I drift into what seems like forever.

I love when the nighttime comes,

and I can drift away.

In those moments are when he comes.

Everything about him feels right.

Everything about this moment

is meant to last a lifetime.

I am here as he lies beside me

whispering to my soul

while our spirits run free.

#17:

_____

I ask of you this one thing.

Be brave enough

to stand beside me

and hold my hand.

Be fearless enough

to stand strong

and not run at the first sight

of who I really am.

#18: _____

He has invaded my thoughts,

a territory that was never his.

I have become a captive

in my own thoughts.

I don't want to think about him,

but I do.

I don't want to like him,

but dammit I feel him everywhere.

He has found his way inside my heart

and I must let him go.

There is no more us and we will never be.

We are just stolen moments in time,

when our spirits meet, intertwine,

and then part from one another.

#19: _____

Love will take it all.

It will take everything

and break your heart.

So, I'm packing it up,

and I'm going to put it somewhere

they cannot reach.

I'll pack it in that old box

where I put all my memories

I try to forget and push it to the back.

Since they never plan

to stay for long,

it's better this way.

You learn a thing or two

when your heart

becomes a revolving door.

And I've learned it is better

to let them leave.

Therefore, I patiently wait

for distance

to move between us

and make itself at home.

#20: _____

I would give you something,

a small piece of myself,

so I am not left empty,

and you would still leave me

with nothing to hold on to.

You have the power to remove

just a little bit

to feed the insatiable desire

you have for me,

but you leave with all my sanity

and all my love knowing

that's all that is keeping me alive.

You selfish motherfucker.

#21: _____

Buyer's remorse forces me

to regret making

a home inside your heart.

I nestled my way

within in its lining,

covering myself

with its warmth.

I hung pictures of us

on its walls to show you

I was here to stay.

I created a place

of comfort and safety

for both of us to reside.

I threw away the keys to doors

leading to other lovers.

Lovers, we had no room for

in this space we now shared.

I got comfortable

because this is where

I thought I'd be forever.

Foolishly, I made a home

inside of your heart,

territory no longer feeling

like home.

A place once filled with

comfort & safety,

and I've been trying

to find my way out

since the day you let her in.

#22: _____

I wonder if I really gave you

all my love,

would it be enough for you?

Would you have everything

you need to love me,

or would you still require more

and leave me with nothing

left to give myself?

#23: _____

I want to erase him from

my memory before the insanity sets in.

Before the fixation becomes unbearable

and I am no longer able to fight it off.

I want to extricate him from

the essence of my soul

before he settles within its layers

and makes himself at home.

Life is a bitch and love

has become the mechanism

he uses to constantly turn me out.

#24: _____

She can only love who she wants to love

and he is who she desires.

He is the hurt she is running from,

as the lust that seeps from

his skin draws her in.

She falls, weakened to the obsession

she tries to fight.

Temptation is a weakening antidote

she yearns to taste and be free of.

#25: _____

I want to remove these thoughts of you,

and place them somewhere

they can never be found.

I want to go on as if you never existed.

My heart has become too familiar with you

and I feel that it is best this way.

My thoughts have already become

consumed by you.

I need to find a way to regain control

before it becomes too late.

#26: _____

I feel you within me,

still I am not able to let you stay.

There is something magnificent

and powerful about you.

Maybe it's the familiarity

that is nestled between us,

or the fire that somehow

keeps both of us burning.

We are different, yet we are alike.

Tragic, but somehow beautiful.

#27: _____

Time changes things, including love.

Everything begins so sweet,

then ends so unpleasant.

I remember when we called this love.

Now it has become something

I fight daily to move pass.

It still believes in you.

It still believes in me,

and it is determined to fight.

I love that it remembers you

and still wants to keep a part of you,

but for the pieces of my heart

that haven't turn their back on me,

this love can no longer be.

#28:

Today,

obsession laid idle

& absurdity periodically

frolicked amongst my thoughts.

I want no part of them,

however,

my spirit lives off

their very existence.

I often wonder can love appear

within the infatuation

I have for you.

Then reality always reminds me

of the source in which

I seek love from,

and I am right back

to where we started.

#29: _____

My soul seeks love buried in places

it knows it will never surface from.

I believe my spirit craves lust

since the existence of love

is so hard to grasp.

I know one day

it will eventually manifest,

but for now, I will hide

within my thoughts of fascination

and chaotic madness.

#30: _____

It seems like yesterday

has repeated itself once again.

Today the absence of you

brings this unbearable silence,

and this excruciating pain

I can't seem to shake.

How can one thing

be easily replaced with another?

Why does this victory feel like defeat?

How is that I decided to let you go,

but my body is still holding on?

Where do I begin with trying to forget you?

I loved you, but that wasn't good enough,

and now we are finished.

#31: _____

The madness often creeps in and

chaos has her way with me.

I want this fascination I have for you

to evolve into love,

but I fear it may never be.

My heart cries out for you,

but my soul is contempt

with the lust you choose to give.

#32: _____

I think about yesterday

and then I think about tomorrow.

All the while forgetting about today.

I remember how I would get lost

in your eyes and the mysterious soul

that lies behind them.

I smile at how I can never

get the past back.

No matter how hard

I close my eyes and wish for

yesterday, it will never come back to me.

I want to know are you

haunted by the memories that haunt me.

Are you consumed by these feelings

I am drowning in?

Do you ever feel conflicted

about all the wrong doing

and times that we hurt each other?

I remember the good times.

I relish in the times you made me smile,

and then instantly

the bad memories creep back in

and anger wins all over again...

#33: _____

I want to remember the nights

we held each other,

but the lonely ones

have become dominate

in the forefront of my mind.

I don't know what this feeling is,

though I am familiar with

how those days will never return,

and tomorrow will come

whether I want it to or not.

So today and the memories

that came with it

are what I'll hold onto.

#34: _____

There is something about him

I can't resist.

I am unable to possess him,

still I want him.

I want the erotic, harmonious

melody his heartbeat creates

when love is fighting the hardest.

The rare moments,

when passion has set in

and everything else

is thrown out of the window.

I have this undiscovered allure

that secretly drives me

to always wanting him.

I want so badly to hear

his heartbeat against mine.

I am infatuated with him.

I know he is probably no good for me,

but it doesn't stop me from constantly

finding my way back to him.

And this time, I'm holding on for dear life.

#35:

_____

Misplaced ideals are dangerous

when you build a fantasy

around them.

My allegiance had always been

given to you without any proof

you wanted to be here.

I was in love with the idea of us.

In love with ideas and ideals,

while ignoring the signs

& the signals

& the realities

blaring loudly.

I was head over heels for us

though not who we really were,

but who I saw us to be

in the circumference of my mind.

I was loyal to those ideas

because I believed

you would somehow become

what I'd dreamed you would be

& prayed you would be

while comparing our horoscopes

& compatibility charts

& anything that aligned

with my ideas of who

I'd created us to be.

Buried deep in the

layers of my imagination,

we were in love

& happy

& living this blissful life

I wanted to have so badly.

But that's not who you are,

that's not who you chose to be.

Today, I'm breaking up

with those ideas

& dreams

& fantasies

that won't let me be

and finding truth in my reality.

#36: _____

My passion for you

has eluded my judgment

in the worst way.

This feeling, this moment,

has somehow taken over us.

But you don't feel the same way

as I do,

and once again,

my need for you

has gotten the best of me.

I listen to your thoughts.

I absorb the things you to say to me.

The words fall harshly upon my ears,

and I beg my heart to avoid

inhaling the things, you say.

They are sugar-coated with shallow love,

there is no depth within them.

Breathing them in would only

give them room

to float around,

to disrupt my soul,

& the love story I need to survive.

#37: _____

I look at you.

I see a man I know I can love,

while begging for him

to love me back.

Our love began as a secret

and you feel it must remain one.

I plead with the future

to give me one, single moment

to say you are mine.

I bargain with time to make

you see how perfect we could be.

Love cannot be my recourse

since time does not care.

Today is not interested in me

loving you,

tomorrow will be the same.

#38.

It amazes me that even a glimpse

of your heartbeat

can make me smile.

I want to always know

what it's like to exist in your world.

A world that allows you and I to be one.

Wherever you are I am & will always be.

I love to capture your gaze,

and hold it hostage.

I've tried to think of someone else,

breathe someone else in,

absorb their energy,

but no one feels as good as you.

You are an addiction that has taken over,

causing me to submit to anything.

I want nothing else but to feel you inside me.

I have acknowledged you are lunacy

I no longer want to be cured of.

#39: _____

Damn,

I hate that you have

invaded my body.

I hate that all

I want is to feel the heat

from your soul.

I respire to relieve the tension

my heart has taken on.

The insides of my walls beg

to feel a piece of you

if not all of you.

I crave you

and nothing else other than you

will feed this habit I have

become dependent on.

#40: _____

Conscious nightmares

eat away at me.

Subconsciously I can't

forget about you,

but consciously the memory

of you no longer exist.

My mind is in this constant state

of rescuing a memory

I've tried to kill over-and-over,

and all I want is to stop

being a prisoner in my own mind.

#41: _____

Somewhere between

meeting you,

holding you,

fucking you,

and loving you,

I fell victim to

what we were meant to be,

what we once were,

what we would no longer be.

I'm still living in those instants.

Still caught in this purgatory

of he's coming back,

& bitch he's long gone,

while fighting like hell

to find myself once more.

#42: _____

I want so bad
to hold you right now.
To smell your scent,
to feel your hands
caress the inside of my thighs.
To get lost in the intoxication
of your kisses,
but time and distance,
right and wrong,
the vows you said to her,
the lies you told me,
prevents those moments
from occurring.
Maybe, just maybe
time will allow us to steal
a few moments of each other
we don't have to pay for.

#43: _____

There is something impossible about you.

Something that rights all wrongs,

curing even the slightest hint of pain.

But there is something,

a piece of space,

dividing us and will not let us be.

Perhaps, time can see the hurt,

the mistakes,

the regret,

that may come from this love,

or maybe this is not love at all.

#44: _____

You are in a place I cannot reach.

This quiet obsession

I have over you is screaming

within the walls of my mind.

I have tried to extract you,

purge you from the corners

of my unstable heart,

& the fortifications of my soul,

but a piece of you

is always left behind.

I want to be free of you

as you are me.

My existence is so fused with you

and I need an escape.

I breathe you out,

but your intoxicating scent

penetrates my senses

and I manage to inhale you

all over again.

#45: _____

You don't love me anymore,

& I don't love you,

but we keep holding on.

We keep tightening the grip

on the other's heart.

We keep the jerking the chains

we've shackled to our feet,

unable to relinquish this need for control.

This love has come crashing down,

the pieces are thrown everywhere.

But you keep cutting me,

and I keep cutting you.

We continue to

destroy each other's love,

knowing we have no real desire

to be with one another.

When does it end?

When do we find the strength

to let this go?

When do we stop cutting

ourselves long enough

to find a way to let the other heal.

#46: _____

I have no idea how my heart feels,

or how to truly heal a broken heart.

There is no beat,

there is no sound,

there isn't the slightest indication

it is still functioning.

It's tired,

worn & beaten down.

It wants no part of this

artificial love circulating

and neither do I.

I want to wake up

& every thought of you,

be a distant second in time.

Every ounce of you purged

from the arteries flowing

to my heart,

never having to existed.

This way nothing will hurt anymore.

This way I won't have to relive

heartbreak another day.

#47: _____

I don't know who I am anymore,

or what I am becoming.

I don't want to breathe without you,

but my lungs are unable to inhale you.

Every part of me aches for you,

yearns for you,

craves you,

but out of fear of consumption,

& addiction,

& heartbreak,

& sadness,

my soul, it won't allow me

anywhere near you,

and I know it's safer this way.

#48: _____

You are embedded

at the very core of my soul,

yet love will not allow us to be.

It does not trust us with one another.

It fears we are too irresponsible

with its feelings.

I want to hold you.

I want to be free of you.

It seems I constantly close a door

I know I will soon open again.

#49: _____

Warning signs rarely ever

appear to be

important until they are.

I knew who he was,

what he could do,

what he'd become.

He always seemed like

a heartbreaker.

The kind that stuck with you

for a long time.

The very specimen

accompanied with feelings,

latching onto you

and burying themselves

in places you didn't know

heartache could hide in.

He was the brand of misery

your body would betray

your heart for time-after-time.

The type who implanted himself

into the lining of your lungs,

the marrow of your bones,

the crevices of your spine,

stretching,

& molding,

& hiding himself

deep enough to go undetected.

He was never the version

that acted like a stranger

in an unknown place.

He was indeed a heartbreaker

that made a home inside my heart.

The kind that had warm eyes,

a forgiving smile,

and a love that would take you

years to recover from.

#50: _____

I leave my feelings for him where we lay

because I know my heart

will not permit me to leave with them.

The risk of heartbreak is too great.

I must enjoy them,

enjoy him,

enjoy us,

within our embezzled moments.

I hear his heartbeat as I lay

upon his warm skin

and I become mesmerized with its sound.

I wonder what makes it beat.

I wonder if I am buried within its walls.

I wonder if I will ever have a chance

to savor a part of him

somewhere other than here,

or if we will always be a

right here, right now lie.

LOVE, HEARTBREAK, AND HANGOVERS

#51: _____

This time was the last time.

It's what it told myself

to justify all the nights

I lost sleep & time,

& tears and moments,

I could never have back.

So last night I dug a hole

and I put us in it.

I buried us far beneath

the heartache running

rampant amongst us.

I hid what was left of our love.

I hid it from heartache.

I hid it, so we could do

nothing else to break us.

But like the many times before,

when you weren't looking,

I found myself selfishly saving

a piece of the good remaining,

just in case we'd ever have

a chance at love again.

I dug a hole last night,

and I put some of us in it.

I did it because I loved us

and so, we could finally run

and find something better.

#52: _____

There is something that lies here,

the unknown that lies between us.

We see it, but we deny it.

We want it,

though we refuse to reach for it.

The loss of freedom scares us

to the point of admitting

we belong together.

I try to capture love,

but it runs fast to be free.

#53: _____

We always find ourselves skin to skin,

heartbeat to heartbeat.

Excepting that gravity continues

to push us together,

we breathe each other's air.

But like always,

pride and the fear of rejection keeps us

from speaking our truth.

Past heartache forces us to suppress

how we really feel.

One day, we will ignore pride

and overcome fear.

Someday, heartache won't be our story.

One day, we will allow ourselves

a chance to love the way we should.

#54: _____

I have no room left

in my thoughts that

revolve around you.

No space remaining for

the occupancy of your bullshit,

or the capacity to revive a life

that has since died.

Time has taken ahold of me,

and there is none left for me

to share with memories of you.

#55: _____

Reminders of

every one-night stand,

& every late-night call,

& every pretend whisper

of I love you,

& every song reminding me

of what I lost,

& every tease of the cologne

that once made me weak,

& every gentle breeze

I mistake for your touch,

& fingertips that once

grazed my skin,

& the brushes against strange lips

in hopes one of them

feels like what once was

& the abandoned shirt I now sleep in

hanging on the door,

& the toothbrush I can't throw away,

& the strange imprints

on my sheets I can't wash out.

These memories I fight nostalgia for

are buried in all the stand in lovers

I tried to make a home out of.

All of them as temporary

as the moments shared with

what I thought looked like love.

#56: _____

This thing we call love

has become an infection

that has contaminated our souls,

and we don't know how

to cleanse ourselves of it.

We keep slowly killing each other,

but we are happily unhappy.

#57: _____

They say leaving is a sign of strength.

It proves you can stand on your own.

They also say fleeing a toxic relationship

is better than staying,

but how can that be true?

How can anything feel worse

than the loneliness I am feeling?

Is it even possible for anything

to be more horrific

than the voices screaming in my head,

the cracking of my heart,

the pull-and-tug of exhaling him?

No, nothing could possibly feel this bad,

nothing could possibly break my heart

faster than me leaving him, so I'm here.

One day, I will leave.

One day, I will be strong enough.

But today is not that day.

Today I need his love to survive.

#58:

I want to smile again.

I want to know the sound

of passion.

I want to see curiosity

at its most innocent moment.

I want to embrace love.

I want love to want me.

When my heart heals,

I know love will come again.

#59: _____

You whisper in my ear

and for a minute,

for a millisecond,

you & I seem like we're going to be ok.

No broken hearts, nights of crying,

and traces of loneliness

could ruin this moment.

We are as separate as we are together,

and I cope with the fact we are not meant to be.

I love this tragedy as much as I love you,

and I have no idea how to be free.

#60: _____

I sit and reminisce

about all the nights

we have stolen from time,

all the instances we cheated love.

I wonder will we ever

need to pay them back,

or if we'll ever be punished

for taking what was never ours?

I want to own the moments

I spend with you.

I need to have a memory

that doesn't end in sadness.

I am no longer satisfied

with borrowed love & time.

#61: _____

The sacrifices

we made in the name of love,

only to realize it was never love.

We want to be embraced

by love so bad,

we get lost in its lies instead

of standing in its truth.

Seeing you again reminded me

of the truth,

the realities,

the life,

I wanted to explore

without the compromises,

and excuses made for it.

Oh, how I

remember the innocence

& warmth of love.

How it felt before it

became ruined by you.

#62: _____

Make me your #1.

For once choose me.

Let me feel what it's like

to take precedence

within your feelings.

I want to feel like I matter

to someone,

to you and there is possibly,

an ounce of space

for me in your crowded heart.

Say that you love me just once.

Grant my desperation this

one wish.

I need to know what it feels

like to bask in the glow

of being first in someone's eyes.

#63: _____

One day,
love will stop laughing
at me,
and I will not be the one
standing alone.
Love will pick me up
and smile at me.
It will greet me like
an old friend.
It will convince me
to believe in it again.
One day,
love will prove to me
it always wins.

#64: _____

For a split second,

I remembered you.

I remembered your smile,

your touch,

& the sound of your voice

that held my ears hostage

each time you whispered in them.

I remembered the way

you kissed me,

and even said goodnight.

I remembered all the times

you always

made me feel as if nothing

or no one else existed.

Whenever the weight of the world

was on my shoulders,

when all was lost,

and the bottom was falling out,

I tried to remember love

& I fought to remember you.

#65: _____

I miss you.

I try not to miss you,

but my unrequited thoughts

always travel back to you.

I have forced myself into

forgetting you,

still a part of me

keeps you hidden away

for quiet moments,

and safe keeping,

when I need to feel you near.

I know that we can never be,

but the delusion of it all

keeps me alive.

#66: _____

My smile is nothing more

than a disguise

for the civil war going on inside

of my heart.

A brutal war that the brokenness

left behind is determined to win.

It's merely a mask,

an illusion,

possibly a hallucination,

to misdirect the silent deconstruction

my ribs are feeling

from the pressure

my broken heart makes as it tries

to escape.

My smile, though bright,

warm, and welcoming is a camouflage

to hide the darkness my soul

has been swallowed by.

This smile I am forced to smile

is a personification of happiness,

I have embraced to deter the tears

my eyes are on the edge of releasing.

My smile, is not really a smile.

It is an upward movement of my lips

sitting at the corners of my face

to hide the screaming,

& the crying,

& the breaking,

& the hurting

I am doing inside.

#67: _____

There's no secret to love,

yet people somehow

make it seem like there is.

Everyone always tells you

to love with your whole heart,

but no one tells you how

to love when pieces go missing.

No one sticks around

long enough to give you more

fucking unsolicited advice

about a feeling that hits you

like a ton of bricks.

No one tells you to hold on

tight as the rollercoaster

takes off at a speed

you are in no control of.

They tell you to fall in love

freely, but they never tell you

there will come a time

when you need a parachute,

a soft place to land,

a back-up plan,

because this beautiful thing

is going to pull the rug

from under your feet

and you are going to collapse so hard,

pieces of you are going to fall everywhere.

They say love with your whole heart,

yet, no one stays around

long enough to tell you which pieces

you are supposed to love with.

#68:

I wish I could erase

ever feeling your lips

on my skin,

or the heat we created

when our bodies touched.

Love is so cruel,

and time is its evil partner.

The longing for you

has driven me to the brink

of insanity's edge.

I want to make you disappear,

but your memories find comfort

in the walls of my mind.

Replacing the thought of you

only affords me

temporary pleasure,

before reality

reappears again.

#69: _____

Ecstasy waves rip
through my body
and I scream as loud
as desire & pleasure
will allow me to.
I search for tears,
but my heart will not
allow me to cry over him.
I try to curse his name,
but my tongue refuses
since it would be in vain.
I love him.
I live for him.
I crave him.
I worship him.
But I want him to leave me
and my delicate heart alone.

#70: _____

UNREQUITED LOVE

is the worst kind of love

to possess,

to be engulfed in,

to be subdued by.

It's the kind of love

that diminishes slowly

before your eyes.

It pulls you apart

muscle by muscle,

limb by limb,

exposing who you really are.

It's the kind of love

that forces you

to die a slow death

as it eats away

at the insane parts

of you fighting to hold onto

the clinically sane parts of you

trying to let go.

This love I have,

this love you have left me

alone in is

a tortuous burden

to carry,

to possess,

to be immersed in.

We both know

I need to let you go.

We both know

I need to fall out

of love with you.

We both know

I am not strong enough

to hold on any longer.

All I ask is for you to

believe in me,

tell me I can do it.

Please, I need you to

give me a chance to try.

#71: _____

He never promised he would stay.

He never said this was real.

Drunken words

whispered during sex cannot

be taken to heart.

When the morning appears

and the sun shines on our faces,

names and love,

are things long forgotten.

#72: _____

Never fall for someone

when you don't know

who they really are,

or have a glimpse into

who they may become.

Love is a deafening emotion,

but loyalty,

loyalty is a crippling effect guilt

uses to paralyze you.

I am not responsible

for the sins they are held down by,

and the skeletons they cleverly hide.

I am not to blame for

walking out on demons,

I never knew existed.

Loyalty can kiss my ass.

#73: _____

Letting go is an acquired taste.

One I am unfamiliar with.

One minute I want to taste

every follicle that makes up

your majestic skin,

while on the other

I want to wash you

from the lining of my lips.

Internally I have become

accustomed to how you function

within my system.

Knowing you are the unhealthiest

form of love I should let in,

I keep doing it.

I keep swallowing the lies,

& the lust

& the lonely nights

& the morning sadness,

after consuming too much

of something I have

convinced myself is love.

Repeatedly partaking of

dose after dose,

spoonfuls of what is essentially

no good for me.

I want to savor freedom.

I want to relish

in the afterglow of what love

truly feels like.

I want to taste mouthfuls

of letting you go

until you become a flavor

my palette no longer thirsts for.

#74: _____

His kisses were incentives

for me to give

him what I convinced myself

would be forever.

This love he swore we shared

only existed in the corners of my mind.

His words were always laced

with promises of forever.

The imprint on his finger,

the momentary highs of pleasure,

and the late-night goodbyes,

proved his forever belonged

to someone else.

#75: _____

I'm going to be the one

who hurts you first.

This way I don't have to give

the pillows my tears at night,

or the morning my excuses

for why I'm going to take you back

after you hurt me

for what I tell myself is the last time.

#76: _____

I have accepted living in hell
because what may await me
on the other side of this door
terrifies the shit out of me.
I have mastered the art
of masking pain disguised as love,
hurt portrayed as happiness.
The many faces I am forced
to embody and depict
to make it just one more day
of not being alone.

#77: _____

Your heart is a unicorn.

It's magic to them,

but you know how it works.

Everyone won't respect it

so, protect your light.

Protect your methods.

Protect your inspiration.

Protect your happy.

Protect your goddamn heart.

Don't be closed off,

but I beg you, do be mindful.

Be mindful of what

pieces of yourself

you choose to reveal,

you choose to share.

Never too much.

Never too soon.

#78: _____

Our sins are served up on a silver platter

as we dine at the table of lies

and deceit we've set for one another.

We swallow lust whole,

allowing the bitterness

to nestle itself in the lining of our mouths,

while love fights to escape

the madhouse we've built around it.

#79: _____

I chose to love you in silence.

For in silence there was no rejection,

no hurt,

no right or wrong.

I chose to love you in my dreams.

For in my dreams,

no one belongs to you but me.

#80: _____

Please say you don't remember

that one time I said I love you

and I wasn't particularly sure I did,

but I let it fall from my lips

and it fell, slowly, but it fell

onto your earlobes

and you begged me

never to say it again.

Your voice, it wasn't harsh,

but the way you said it

made me feel afraid.

Afraid I wasn't certain,

afraid I was entirely sure,

afraid this wasn't a safe place

for whatever truths we

wanted to embrace.

I couldn't understand

why you said it or if it was

what I'd expected to hear,

but you begged me so many times

not to say it again.

I wasn't sure if you were afraid

I didn't love you

or if you didn't feel the same.

Many nights I lie awake

remembering that one time

I said I loved you and you never,

ever said you felt the same.

I remember.

I remember.

I remember,

but please tell me you don't,

so one day I can find the courage

to say it to someone again.

#81: _____

Baby,

you'll drove yourself insane

searching for the good

in a man who ain't shit.

It's unhealthy.

It's maddening.

Its disordered turmoil designed

to leave you empty,

and my heart has been

bled completely dry.

#82: _____

This bleeding heart of mine

opens & closes

& expands,

& shrinks,

constantly,

yet not enough,

and sometimes too much

when it comes to you.

It searches for you,

& hides from you,

& reaches for you,

& runs from you,

while trying to find

its purpose,

& reason,

& role in your life.

Sadly, my bleeding heart

doesn't know when to quit

& leave,

& say goodbye,

& throw in the towel,

because it always opens

& closes,

& expands,

& shrinks too much,

yet not enough for you

to ever leave.

#83: _____

My lips still have

the remnants of your

taste upon them.

The sweetness of your kiss

lingers on my tongue

like a long-lost lover

as I savor & swallow

the ecstasy

I reach every time

you're close.

#84: _____

Her beautiful brown skin

draped her body as the

black & blue

senselessness

surrounded the sadness

her eyes held.

Disappointment

smothered her face.

She was covered in the

idea of forever

while suffering in the stigma

she believed was true love.

#85: _____

He fell in love with her unruliness.

The pieces of her that were broken

and able to be controlled.

He reveled in the

bedlam she thrived within,

the dependency that stroked his ego.

Though, now that she has stepped

into the light,

now that she has found herself,

he fears she will no longer be his to control.

#86:

I blew up my life for him.
I risked everything
and he left me standing alone,
left me falling in the open air.
Abandonment became the force
that caught me,
and held on tight,
wrapping itself around my heart.

#87: _____

His fear was that she would

one day wake up

and see that she deserved more.

More than his madness.

More than his abuse.

More than the shame of his infidelity.

More than the subpar love

he was giving her every day.

#88:

I often think about this, about us.

About this feeling we call love.

Was it ever really love or was that what we felt

we should call it at the time?

Has it always been there

or did it find its way here over time?

I don't know if we will ever move passed this

or if this is the end of our chapter.

#89: _____

You're not the hero in this story.

You're not the one who saves the day

and rescues me from this life

of mine going up in flames.

You don't get to kick down the walls

you forced me to build around my heart.

I don't need the lifeline you extend

to ease your guilt.

You're not my savior

despite the fact I need to be saved.

This time, you don't get to whisk me

away from the heartache

you caused like a knight in shining armor.

This time, you are the villain

in our tales of love & torrid affairs,

and the princess saves herself.

#90: _____

Today I tried not to miss him.

I was strong until the sun went down,

and the coolness of the night settled in.

I truly miss him, and I don't want to.

Part of me yearns for him to call,

to say he's sorry again,

to tell me he loves me once more,

and we move past this.

Then the other part begs

me to finally let him go,

screams fuck him girl,

and tells me to keep it moving.

I thought we were getting better.

I felt this time would be different.

Love can be so tricky.

He was the love I thought I wanted,

the future I convinced myself I needed.

Today I missed him.

Hopefully, tomorrow will be different.

#91: _____

Olivia Pope is my name.

Not my real name,

but he calls me Olivia Pope,

and in many ways, I am.

Not in the I save the day kind of way,

but the why am I a hoarder

of broken things,

things that are not my own,

things I have been hypnotically drawn

to with no recourse as to how

they may damage me kind of way.

Why do I have this innate,

& ingrained,

& dire need to fix things

& people who are not interested

in being fixed.

How is it possible I constantly

gravitate towards emotionally,

defective hearts I am fully aware

cannot reciprocate

the kind of love I need.

How have I gone this long

with this incurable disease,

and not see that maybe I am

the emotionally broken heart

that needs to be fixed?

How have I not been able to see

maybe I'm not protagonist

in these heroic tales after all.

Maybe I am the one who needs

to be fixed,

& rescued,

& saved.

#92: _____

I always told myself I was not

like those other girls.

I didn't want to be another love story

told over time.

I could not fathom being written

in history like Juliet,

& Julius Caesar,

clinging to a lover

that was never any good for me.

I am a wild woman

with an unbridled spirit.

A gypsy soul unfamiliar with

planting roots in places meant to last.

I am not the kind of woman

you make a home out of.

I will never be the type of girl

who waits for you to turn your key

after a long day of work.

My heart was never meant to be

a place someone stayed in

for prolonged periods of time.

But he has chained himself

to my love

& my soul,

& my hands,

& the walls of my mind.

And the tragedy of it all

is that I don't want to ever

be free of him.

#93: _____

I wanted to love him
but he could not trust that love,
he couldn't believe in that love.

I wanted to love him,
but he could never reciprocate
that love,
and I can't make him love me
if he won't.

#94: _____

I *dream* of you.

Not because I want to

but because your face is implanted in my mind.

His hands remind me of yours.

The way he kisses me makes me want you.

I am imprisoned in a life I no longer want.

This love no longer seems to fit me.

I have stepped outside of myself,

and I am unable to return to the old me.

All I have left are the many

frozen seconds I had with you.

If only you could see me the way I see you.

If for one moment, you could relieve me

of the desperation I am confined in.

#95: _____

Sometimes we get lost,

and lose our way.

I know because I have been lost.

Lost within the hopelessness I buried myself in.

Stuck within the deepest cracks of loneliness.

Though even in my moments of being lost,

& hurt,

& broken,

& scared,

I found my way back to the light.

So, all I ask of you is to forget about me.

Make me the distant thought

I have tried so many times to make you.

I don't want you to love me anymore.

I am no longer strong enough to love you.

#96:

This emptiness we've settled in

no longer refills itself.

The magnetic chemistry that once

pulled us together

becomes a constant hole that grows,

and continues to separate us.

We've replaced the casual mentions

of I love you

with silent breaths,

and sporadic exchanges of contempt.

We find comfort

in being the perfect strangers.

Two people who only exist

to create misery for one another.

My resolve has come to terms

with this nightmare never ending.

It's too late for us, there is no saving this.

We no longer fight to make it work,

cause we don't give a fuck about love.

#97: _____

Simple math ain't always simple.

I add it up in my head, countless times

to make it make sense.

1+1=2,

1+1=2,

1+1=2,

and still with everything,

with all my rationale,

and with all my intellect,

my heart can never

make it make sense.

1+1=2,

1+1=2,

1+1=2,

but it never equals us,

it never adds up to me & you.

#98: _____

The girl I used to be,

she was ready to let go.

She was ready to end it all.

She had to make the decision to live,

to believe she was better than him.

In time, she realized

the good about herself

that was worth saving.

#99: _____

Not loving you hasn't been easy.

It's a part of me.

A part of who I have become,

but I'm tired of this thing,

I'm tired of being this.

This pain that seems to be our story,

your story,

my story for these past five years.

As each day passes, the memories

of you become detached,

& obsolete,

& further from the front of my mind.

Making forgetting about you easier.

Each day I wake up is a new day,

I can finally breathe without

an ounce of YOU pain.

#100: _____

Self-inflicted wounds take longer

to heal because we are blind

to how we are hurting ourselves.

I am in denial about fantasies

that will never be realities,

lies that will never be truth,

lust that will never be love,

& hope that will end in tragedy.

I struggle with them because

I have this unhealthy attachment

with how you love me

and destroy me at the same time.

I'm always shuffling between

fighting less & staying longer.

Both seem to be the demise

and undoing of my heart.

#101: _____

I wanted to harbor you.

Keep you locked away

& buried inside from the world.

I wanted to bury myself inside of you,

in hopes you would manifest

into what I knew you could be.

I wanted to mold you

and the outlandish love you,

and only you could give me.

I soon realized I did to you

the very thing you did to me

and now we are broken.

#102: _____

He touched me in a place

only sorrow resided and found

I was a perfect, catastrophic storm,

wanting so badly to exist in his world.

I was a succubus fighting to breathe

the same air he breathed.

A parasite searching for any

form of love to latch onto.

I believed he was everything

I wanted, only to realize

he was just as broken as I was.

#103: _____

The naive part of me wanted to believe you cared,

but the realistic side of me knew better.

I couldn't believe in you anymore.

I searched for rationale when the truth

was staring me in the face.

I had nothing left to give to what you once were.

I placed you on a pedestal you were undeserving of,

all in the name of what I assumed was love.

#104: _____

My body is numb as my reflection

in the glass stares back at me.

The idea of love existed,

though the actual form of love

never resided between us.

I ingest the only thing

that makes me forget he hasn't come

home again.

I give my soul the solace it needs

to forgive my heart,

and make peace with my mind.

Holding onto what I inevitably

need to let go of will only continue

to break my fragile heart.

#105: _____

Love and I

have never been friends.

Just strange lovers

meeting by chance.

We've always had forbidden moments,

never lasting memories,

to evolve over time.

One day,

I will forgive love.

Eventually, but no time soon,

I will open my arms to the possibility

of it being a part of my life again.

Until then,

we will carry on as strange lovers

trapped in the pleasurable waves

of our chance encounters.

#106: _____

I never had much faith

in love and miracles.

Though hope,

hope has always been

my biggest vice.

Hope has always been

my downfall.

And knowing this,

I press my ear to your lips

hoping to hear something,

anything that will pull me

back from the edge.

A desperate plea,

an intangible echo,

an uncaged outcry

that makes me believe you

want me to stay.

Scream something,

say something,

show me something,

an inkling of hope,

a flicker of possibility,

that keeps me from

walking out on you.

#107: _____

We treat love like it's a casual drug.

Crazed fiends looking for a thrill.

Never anything permanent,

never anything that feels like something real.

We cling to it hoping we will avoid

the inevitable withdrawals of heartache.

Our orgasms temporarily hide it,

fighting to disguise the pain that seeps

through the cracks as truth breaks free.

Momentary highs laced with love

coursing through our veins.

#108: _____

He stretched it,

bent it

and even tried to break it.

He never realized

I had an elastic heart.

Bruised,

and no longer capable of

being broken anymore.

#109: _____

I'm always stitching
myself back together.
My outer core is nothing more
than a sad excuse for armor,
since my insides
are constantly falling apart.
You have always been
a scrapbook of what I
imagined life to be.
A collection of poems
I write over-and-over,
traces of hope I use to
piece together
my good days and bad days,
my moments of love
& fragments of heartbreak.
The countless letters and words
I convey to pull you in
and put myself back

in this crazed cycle of us.

#110: _____

The voices in my head

give life to the memories

of him I try hard to forget.

My dignity that's drowning in

the bottle of Hennessy

reminds me what I feel is real.

I tell myself it will get better.

but no part of me believes the lie.

I tell my heart it won't always be broken,

love won't always feel like this,

but as it repairs itself one more time,

it reminds me we've been here before.

The heaviness of the bottle weighs

on my conscience,

while my tongue anxiously

awaits its next sip.

My body pleads with me

to find another way to cope.

I want to please them all.

My empty heart,

& my used body,

& my disheveled conscience,

but they can never get on

one damn accord.

They can never work together

on how we are supposed to feel.

I swallow more of what I know

will make it all go away.

I savor another sip of

what I pray will silence them all.

#111: _____

The scars were there,

like dents unable to be removed.

The old and the new.

I was a manufacturing catastrophe

made up of compartments of recalled love.

I had become a junkyard

of discarded pieces embedded in me.

Deeply hidden,

and overshadowed by refurbished parts,

masquerading as something new.

A model transformed into someone

I no longer recognized,

as each new scar became

a classic spin on heartbreak.

#112: _____

I refused to keep being vulnerable

to his behavior,

& his excuses,

& the million reasons he'd kept hurting me.

I took back my control.

I forgave him.

It wasn't because I was weak.

It wasn't because I condoned what he did.

My forgiveness came

because I was tired of walking in circles,

tired of going down dead-end streets,

and I had no more energy to give

to a direction I was no longer going in.

#113: _____

We are in this stagnant place.

Caught between who we really are

and who we want to be.

Fighting for a love

that is now a hallucination.

Constantly, trying to make this work

when God has already decided for us.

#114: _____

"She's a storm chaser," they say.
I unconsciously, yet consciously
run after those kinds of storms.
But I can't anymore.
I can't fight the winds or battle the storms.
I can't hold my breath underwater,
hoping you'll save me from this hurricane.
And knowing this,
foolishly, I keep standing here.
Hoping you'll throw me a life raft.
Waiting for you to part the skies,
and return the sunshine you stole.
The rain has become unbearable,
and the shade & gloominess
no longer covers the pain
I've fought so hard to hide.

#115: _____

You're not close enough

to hurt me

anymore,

yet the pain

still finds a way

to disrupt my peace

and

settle in like an old friend.

#116: _____

I've become a steeple at

the neighborhood bar.

A permanent fixture

who drowns my pain in

drink after drink,

and the bartender knows my name.

My name that has no face.

My identity is all wrapped up

in me being the girl

who comes in with her blues

and we sit together.

I bring my heartache with me

and place it on the stool right beside me.

It reminds me of why we are here.

It keeps them away.

The would-be suitors destined to become

future reasons why I sit here,

at this bar with heartache

& sadness drinking next to me.

The liquid forget-me-not I partake of

explodes like confetti in my soul,

washing away what's left of my rationality,

while suffocating the snapping sound

my heart has resorted to as it reminds me

I have failed us once again.

With each drop,

I numb the agonizing,

the painful,

consuming memories of all

the would-be suitors

that lead me to this neighborhood bar

I come to drink my blues away.

#117: _____

Broken hearts

make strange bedfellows,

and I've had my share of them.

Strange faces in the mornings,

Lips, I discovered the night before.

Scents, energies, and imprints,

unfamiliar to my sheets.

Empty eyes filled with uncertainty,

and cold hands wrapped around me

that belong to another lover,

whose name I won't remember.

Yes, broken hearts make strange bedfellows,

but it's the only therapy I can afford.

#118:

He liked the idea

of loving me

but not

the reality

of loving me.

Love was a

tough business

and he

didn't have

enough strength

to muddle

through

the messiness

of me.

#119: _____

This aching feeling in my heart

rebels against my poor decisions.

An intoxicating, bad habit

is all you ever were to me.

An addictive fantasy

I have stupidly succumbed to again.

The unwarranted withdrawals of sex

will eventually remind me

of how this moment is temporary.

When the sex cloud clears,

your emotionless behaviors will prove

these feelings aren't real,

& you don't love me,

& how I will have to battle

the force of forgetting you,

and forgiving myself for falling again.

#120: _____

You made me feel so alive

I forgot how to breathe on my own.

My lungs, no longer anchors

to my heart,

allow me to breathe the air

you breathed with ease.

As I stand here,

fresh lungs and all,

I gasp for that sweet taste of oxygen.

I feverishly search for an ounce of air your betrayal

has not corrupted and exhaled.

#121: _____

Our love was not same.

We were two people

with feelings invested

here

and somewhere

unknown.

We pray to be released from this love,

yet we run back

to the very thing that imprisons us.

Hostages unsure if we want to be free.

Strangers connected,

yet searching for love,

someplace else.

#122: _____

This looks like the end.

You and me, I see us dying

right before my eyes

and though I reach for you,

you slip between my fingers.

I try to revive us,

but the more I breathe on you,

the more I touch you,

you slip further away.

A fallen angel who keeps making me cry.

I wish I was special.

I wish you thought I was special.

I'm holding on,

but you're fighting to be free.

And I don't care if it's hurts.

Maybe this is our moment,

the moment we stop pretending

to be who we weren't meant to be.

I want to be in control.

I don't belong here,

but I don't want to let go.

#123: _____

One of these days,

titles are going to be the death of us.

Labels are going to swallow us whole

and what could be real will be nothing more

than something we decided to call it.

I know because I've been that girl.

Swept up in a title like it was a

shiny, new toy.

A label that defined who we were,

who I was supposed to be,

and what I meant to him,

while stripping me of the identity

I swore I'd never give up.

All in the name of being called

something, a namesake

he called someone else.

I lost myself in four to eight letters

that meant nothing

because he never stood

behind its meaning,

or the relationship

I realized I was all alone in.

#124: _____

I was drowning in his hollowness,

and then he swore he needed me

which gave me the strength

to keep holding on,

to keep fighting for us.

I became trapped in his beliefs,

a victim to his unruly behavior.

I adapted to his unpredictable abuse

and accepted his half ass love,

all in the name of not being alone.

How stupid could I be?

#125: _____

Touch my heart once again.

I need to know you exist.

Breathe on me

just one more time

so I know it was real,

and you were not

a figment of my imagination,

a stranger I may have never met.

#126:

Even naked

we were scared to be ourselves.

We stood stripped

at our most vulnerable point

hiding behind our secrets

and the anarchy

that consumed us both.

#127: _____

He was a pain addict,

and I was only

a habitual line of cocaine.

One hit of me brought

about a fleeting high

not meant to last

until the morning.

I was sex, lust,

a pleasurable high,

an overzealous fantasy

never intending to be love.

#128:

We were wolves in
sheep's clothing.
Frauds he, and I were.
We would paint the
town as
savages dressed up in
glorious misery.
Sharing our false
expectations,
unhappiness, and
issues with love
with all who would
care to listen.
He & I,
were nightmares disguised
as forever.
We were pain
adorned in love

searching for other

souls to taint.

#129: _____

I remember this lost girl

who lived in the most beautiful

house on the street.

She had so much love to give

but no one to give it to.

He never valued her.

He never treated her like

she was worth the world she deserved.

Even though she lived

in that beautiful house,

with her beautiful man,

she often wandered the streets

with no place to call her own.

She was emotionally homeless,

always in search of something,

of someone,

of someplace to call home.

#130: _____

Sometimes I call you.

Just to see if you'll answer.

Just to let you know

I'm thinking of you,

and wanting you to see

my number appear across

your screen.

Yes, it's crazy I know,

but it's me wishing you

would at least pick up

to say I'm okay,

& I miss you too,

& I'm glad you called.

I know you won't,

but I call hoping the phone

will ring, and ring,

silently pleading you'll grant me

an ounce of mercy

before the sound I can't forget

plays throughout my ears.

Praying the tone

of your recorded voice

will cut the lifeline

to this perpetuating ideology

of us I am stuck in.

Forcing me to leave pieces of myself,

and these feelings of inadequacy

of never being what you needed

& what you wanted

& how at times it could be draining

& exhilarating

& consuming

& exasperating for you

to play on repeat.

Sometimes, though not all the time,

I call hoping the phone

will no longer ring

& your number will not

be the same

& the sound of someone

other than you

will put me out of my misery

so, I can finally hit delete.

#131: _____

We were always stuck in this state

of transition.

Never knowing if we were

coming or going.

I looked to you for direction,

but you left me

stranded to find your own way.

#132: _____

In peaks of vulnerability

our demons come out to play.

They dress up for one another

to drink and dance the night away.

They know the truth.

They have long figured out

in our nakedness,

we hide behind the pandemonium,

we have become content in.

And when the morning comes,

they would once again

be concealed behind this

blemish we call love.

#133: _____

We were deserted souls trying

to escape a place,

we had already fled.

Vultures circling and

picking away

at what was left of the

other's soul.

Scavengers searching

for traces

of a lost piece of treasure

not meant to be found.

#134: _____

My scars,

bruises and wounds

are proof that you

once occupied this place.

They are tell-tell signs

that you were

unable to love me.

Evidence that proves I

can survive without you.

#135: _____

I hid you.

Buried you deep enough

I could no longer feel you.

Then like a slow burning fire

you rose quickly

to the surface.

Scorching any good

I had left in me.

Leaving nothing behind

but the hell

I had long forgotten you to be.

#136:

In the wee hours of the night,

you sneak into my dreams

and we share passionate

points in time,

forbidden in the morning light.

We part with tidbits of time,

stolen for ecstasy to dance free.

Unwanted pieces of darkness

borrowed,

as we exhale the promises

we know are lies

whispered before dawn.

#137: _____

This old building is hardly

keeping the pillars of our hearts

together.

There was nothing left to say,

nothing left to hold onto to.

We were walls

holding up an empty space.

Eroded souls

that dwelled within the emptiness

we had become familiar with.

Tarnished fixtures

barely holding up

the structures of this lie.

#138: _____

Today's wilted display of

"I'm sorry" and

yesterday's bouquet of

"please forgive me"

were all that separated us

as the aroma of vodka

inside our glasses,

settled within the walls of our lungs.

We sip the self-control slowly,

as we struggle to manage

the rage ready to break free.

There would be no more fuck you's,

no room left for I'm sorry

to be uttered from our lips.

We were no longer people

who mattered to one another.

We were ghosts existing in a hell

we were unable to walk out of.

#139: _____

We were misfits.

Runaways on the run

with this stolen feeling, we captured

and wrestled with on our own.

Criminals labeled as outlaws

in possession of this illegal thing

we called love.

#140: _____

He wanted to be the electricity

that turned on my stars each night.

The light I needed to find my way

from the dark places my past loves

sought to bury me in.

The flicker of light to show me

he would guide my heart forever.

#141: _____

All we ever want is for someone

to stick around.

Someone not too bougie

to get dirty in our messiness.

A brave soul not afraid

to get cut a few times

as they mend our fragile heart.

All we ever want is for someone

to stick around

and help us weather a storm.

#142: _____

We drive ourselves mad thinking it's okay

to stay in this fucked up relationship,

because we convince ourselves

the next one could be worse than this.

We condition ourselves

into believing the grass isn't greener

on the other side so we stay,

and we stay,

and we stay longer than we should.

We stay not realizing that everyday

a piece of ourselves are lost,

gone missing,

possibly never to return.

We hold on too long until

time is stolen away from true love

and we psych ourselves

into believing that

this is as good as it's going to get.

#143: _____

Love is seeing yourself

completely through

someone else's eyes,

and having the courage to stay

even if the person looking back

at you isn't the picture

of perfection or what you

imagined them to be.

#144: _____

Wave your white flag.

Tell me you want to surrender.

Beg me to capture you.

Give me permission

to plant my flag,

bury myself inside you,

and hide in all the places

you never thought to

let anyone else find.

#145: _____

I want fireworks with you.

The Fourth of July,

New Year's Eve kind of fireworks.

I want the snap, crackle,

and pop moments that will guide us

through troubled times.

I want the happily ever after

no one believes in anymore.

I want forever with you

long after the sky has lit up

and darkness covers our faces.

#146: _____

We do what feel is necessary

to move past this moment.

The bourbon laced words that

spew from your lips are covered

in your version of honesty.

I shield myself behind

the intoxicating feeling

that numbs the daggered pain

you force onto me.

Tomorrow our drunken words

will comfort us once again.

Tonight, our sober thoughts run free.

#147: _____

One mistake and you said

fuck me,

fuck this,

fuck us,

gave up,

and walked out the door.

I guess when it comes to me,

forgiveness has gone out of style.

#148: _____

I weep, and I mourn

the hurt parts of me

I concealed deep.

I dance, and I celebrate

the parts of me that chose

to break free.

I marvel at how you

can only love half of me

as you search to find

and fix the broken pieces

that will once again

make me whole.

#149: _____

I believe everyone

in your life serves a purpose.

Whether it is to break you apart,

or build you up,

their sole reason for existing

in your life

is divine and an ordained destiny.

This is what I tell myself about you.

This rationale is how I cope

with us no longer being together.

The older I get I embrace this process

just little bit more,

and each time, it becomes easier

to say goodbye to heartbreak.

#150: _____

He buries a memory of me

in a photo album

he keeps hidden under his bed.

The album filled with all his past loves

and youthful mistakes.

He remembers the good times,

as he rubs my name etched across his arm.

A flashback of us

finds its way to the front of his mind

as a glimmer from the diamond ring

he bought to propose to me

on our anniversary

catches the light in the corner of his eye.

He lives in the mistake I left him

for day-after-day, night-after-night,

when he smells his sheets,

and my scent is gone.

As he hears my name,

and I'm not there.

When he hums our song,

and the words get caught in his throat.

When he stares at the door,

I will never walk through again.

#151: _____

I want to take

your broken pieces

and hold them hostage

against mine, so I can

know what it feels like

to be whole again.

#152: _____

I was free once.

You were free too.

And then, we had this crazy,

destructive, exasperating idea

we could be one.

And sometimes,

not all the time,

we were two tornadoes

clashing together as one.

We engulfed one another

as we swallowed each other whole.

We thoughtlessly imagined we could

be the calm force

to tame the other's storm,

but all we did was cause more

damage along the way.

#153: _____

I fucked him up on purpose.

I broke him into a million pieces

and rubbed them across my skin.

It wasn't because of anything he did,

or because he didn't love me

the way I needed to be loved.

I fucked him up because chaos,

and insanity,

and dysfunction,

and drama are the only things

that makes me feel alive.

#154: _____

Give me a chance to pick up

the pieces you left me in

before you crack me open

and break me all over again.

Let me find my footing

in this world of instability

before you and heartache

trip me up again.

#155:

Taste me, but carefully.

Then gently swallow me

and allow me to swim

throughout your veins.

Let me dive into the place

where we can inhale

and exhale each other.

Let me gracefully float

around inside you

as the echoes of your

heartbeat serenade me.

Let me backflip in your depth

as your soul moves me in waves.

#156: _____

I wish some of the faith

you had for me you'd saved

for yourself.

I pray one day, some of the love

you wanted to

desperately give me,

you eventually use to

heal your own heart.

#157: _____

Let's freeze these moments.

Enclose them,

and trap them

within the walls of an hour glass.

Hide them away

so life has no way

to corrupt them,

and make them be anything

other than

what they are right now—

happiness.

#158: _____

When heartbreak settled in

and took over me,

I wanted to bang on your door.

I wanted to cry.

I wanted to scream I hate you,

and lay all my feelings at your feet.

I needed you to feel an inkling of the pain

you projected onto me.

I wanted this stench of abandonment

to greet you like a hitman sent

to do my bidding.

I wanted my thoughts to be painted

across your door for everyone to see.

For once I wanted my words to be heard.

#159: _____

We sit like ragdolls

on an open shelf.

Outdated products on display

for everyone to see.

Collecting dust like the untold

words we never said.

Our secrets exposed

as the thick black thread,

begrudgingly holding them

and us together

wears thin over time.

#160: _____

This is how I die,

a slow, torturing death.

Not a physical death,

an emotional death

as the unraveling

of my heart strings

are undone before your eyes.

Ragged threads that are worn,

hung, and pulled each time

by the coming and goings

of men like you.

Men who treat my love

like a garment.

Putting it on

& taking it off

& throwing it in a pile

full of other discarded hearts

you have worn

time and time again.

Shadress Denise

We constantly go through this cycle

of trying to wash off the hurt

 you stained me with

and like every time before,

I let you wear my heart

until it becomes

too uncomfortable

and there is no more room for me.

You put me on,

you take me off,

you wash me clean

and finally, you leave me here

hanging, and waiting for the time

to come when my heart

no longer fits,

and you throw me away.

#161: _____

The only time I feel alive

is when you pull the knife out

and drive it back in,

excruciatingly

close to the edge of my heart.

It's how I know it's still there.

It's how I know it still beats for you.

#162: _____

I need to play his madness

on repeat just one more time.

I desperately need him to pull

on my heart strings so

I can hear the melodic rhythm

I have become comfortable with.

His rhythm and my blues.

My fingers don't play them

the way he used to.

Their fingers can't seem

to learn the tune.

We are unfamiliar with how he plays

his, mine, our painful song.

#163: _____

I question myself a lot when it comes to you.

Why do I continue to entangle

my heart in this web of misery?

Knowing damn well you won't do

anything to set me free.

Why do I keep forcing you to be a hero

when I know you are the villain?

Why do I dive deeper into you?

when it is clear, you won't pull me to safety.

Why do I continue to breathe you in,

and I know the toxicity of your lies,

and your love,

and your touch,

and the million goodbyes,

are killing me from the inside out.

#164: _____

Play me like your old guitar.

The one stored away deep

in the back

with the rest of things,

you have given up on.

Dust me off and give my cords

just one more try.

One more stroke to see

if the songs that used

to make us happy

still sounds the same.

#165: _____

Maybe love and bad guys

are one in the same.

It seems there is always

one that gets away.

I am learning how

to live with that.

I'm learning not

to run after them.

#166:

_____

I get lost in the mirror as I begin

to search for myself.

I lose track of who I

really am as

I search for the girl I

once was before you.

I mourn how that

girl is gone.

I weep for the

woman I have

become.

Someone trapped

between the cracks

that hold together

the shattered

reflection

that glares back at me.

#167: _____

You are the lighthouse I search for

when I am trying to find

my way back to shore.

I look for you

as if you are the North Star,

lighting up the sky

as you guide me back to you.

Your heartbeat is a compass

I follow when I am lost.

Always guiding me,

always pointing me

in the direction of home.

#168:

You always knew how to fuck me well.

Whether you were playing with my heart

or your fingertips taunted my skin,

oh, you fucked me well.

I fell head over heels with how you

meticulously pulled my soul

to the edge of madness,

only to leave me fiending for something

I could never have.

The euphoria was fleeting

but the memory of you remains the same.

Oh, sweet darling,

you always knew how to fuck me well.

#169: _____

It started with one slice here

and one slice there.

Just small reminders to myself,

you were real.

I would cut myself when you called,

when you didn't call,

when you forgot to say I love you,

and when you'd go missing.

I cut myself, deeper each time,

for you to see what you do to me

when I'm hurting,

or lonely,

or in need of love in some capacity.

The slices would heal

and then you would disappear again.

In any instance,

I would open old wounds to prove

to you how entrenched you

were inside of me.

I'd cut myself to bring you back.

I'd cut myself to make you stay.

One slice here and one slice there.

Just small reminders to you

that my love was real.

#170: _____

I remember a time we once knew love.

We were reckless, stubborn

and even cavalier with it at times,

but we knew love.

Now we sit here,

staring at each other

as the magnitude

of what we once had separates us.

We once knew love

but now all we have is a recollection.

#171: _____

You remind me of lemonade.

Initially sweet,

& satisfying,

& tart,

to the taste.

The ultra-sweet flavors

of you dance on my tongue,

and *ohhhh* how quickly

I am reminded of the days

we enjoyed & appreciated

the presence of one another.

Then as the sweetness fades,

I swallow the bitterness,

and the realities

of who you truly are.

A mixture of the good

and bad we had become.

#172: _____

She imagined herself
to be loved by him.
She imagined herself
to be needed by him.
She dreamt,
& pleaded,
hoped and wished
she could be anything
other than what she really
was to him.
She wanted to be more than
his 2 a.m. call.

#173: _____

With each drop

that touches my lips,

a piece of me is lost

swimming,

floating,

and eventually drowning,

within the bottle.

As my liquor diminishes,

and my memories

temporarily fade,

my demons rest their hands

on my shoulders

to remind me they are still here.

I hear their whispers

as guilt finds shelter

next to my heartache.

With each sip,

I drink a little bit more.

Washing them away

until there are no memories
of you left.

#174: _____

Like a tattered gown

meant for only you,

my dear,

you wear sadness well.

You dance intimately

with heartbreak

and find comfort

in disappointment.

You hold regret as tight

as a new lover,

hoping it won't betray

& abandon you like the others did.

Though there is a piece of you

that is still alive.

A piece of your heart

that refuses to die.

A small fraction of hope

that knows one day my dear,

you will find something new,

something beautiful to wear

and it will fit you well.

#175: _____

My heart speaks of you

as it remembers secrets untold.

My heart remembers you

as it whispers

stories that proved to be unknown.

My heart bleeds for you

as it fights to carry on.

My heart walks away from you

as it gives up on my soul.

#176: _____

We came to the table

with the intent

of this lasting forever.

Our suitcases were placed

in the corner,

full of the things

we wanted to forget.

Then one day

we opened them,

pulling out everything

we had hidden away.

An arsenal of hurt

we saved for a rainy day,

in case forever

became a lost cause

we no longer spoke of.

#177: _____

Touch me

in places that no man

has been able to reach.

Speak words

into my ears that causes

me to feel things

in places other than

between my legs.

Arouse me

so I crave you

like a habit

only known to junkies.

Make my soul come

so that I can feel

orgasms in the crooks

of my mind.

#178: _____

There will always

be a part of me

that finds peace

and contentment

with living

in our brokenness.

I survive on it.

I understand it.

I trust that it

will always be there,

even when you aren't.

Then there is a part of me

that yearns to be whole.

A fraction of myself

aching to run away

and give my heart

a fighting chance,

to heal the pieces, you broke.

#179: _____

All I ever wanted

was for us to be together.

To dance wildly

in our truths,

leaving behind

the past that seemed

to always make us

miss that next step.

All I ever wanted

was all of you.

The version of yourself

you could never

resist giving to her.

#180: _____

You manipulate feelings

I keep hidden away.

Stirring them to see

what reactions

I am capable of.

You evoke emotions

I shy away from

in the name of

maintaining my sanity.

You are not afraid

to touch the rawness

of who I really am

as you stroke

the monster I hide within.

#181: _____

I wanted you to feel like home.
I forced you to be something
you were not ready to be
and I am reminded of that
as I roam the long,
and lonely hallways,
we have abandoned.

Pictures have been removed
and all that remains
are the nails that
once displayed happy times.
The clinking of glass hanging
from the rusted chandelier
echoes throughout the walls
and for a minute, for a brief second,
I hear sounds of yesterday's laughter.

As I say goodbye, I walk pass a mirror

and see an image of a ghost,

a replica that looked like me,

a love that died,

an afterthought that faded

the moment you walked out the door.

#182: _____

Her God hears

her tears at night.

He wipes

her whimpers away

as he rubs

her back and soothes

her heart.

He whispers forgiveness

in her ears as

she constantly gives

her body

to this undeserving man

that disrupts her soul.

#183: _____

You are danger,

yet I still walk towards you.

A blazing fire

I know will burn me,

and somehow,

I need you to keep warm.

My lifeline,

slowly draining me.

My lifeboat with holes

I find myself constantly plugging,

as I do all I can to keep us alive.

#184: _____

You are terrifying to me.

Your scars paralyze

the fear I hide behind.

The transparency

of your nakedness

gives my vulnerability

room to be free.

Your truth welcomes me

and I recognize,

& embrace,

& embody,

the magic that is you.

#185: _____

I wanted those moments with you.

The memories of you running behind me

as laughter filled both of our ears.

The flashbacks of you telling me

everything was going to be ok.

The nights you would hold my fragile heart

as you dried my cries.

I needed just a moment to feel like

I was somebody's world.

To taste sweet, pure love

as daddy's little girl.

#186: _____

Why don't we break

the curses of those

who came before us.

Why don't we free the lies,

the secrets,

and the mistakes

made by generations

of those preceding us

who abused love.

Let us heal the wounds

that constantly break open

because pain

is what we are accustomed to.

How about we fix each other

this one last time,

sealing up the scars

our past left behind.

#187: _____

When you truly love

someone,

you don't stand in the way

of their dreams,

of their hopes,

of the things keeping them alive.

You make sure

their wings are secure,

their foundation is strong,

their heart is in one piece,

and they know

you are a soft place

to land when they fall.

You wish them well

and you give them

a small push

to help them fly away.

Stop grieving the lost souls

who don't love you,

who don't support you,

who clipped your wings

and left you falling

with no soft place to land.

#188:

When did we decide

to give up on one another?

When did we decide

this wasn't worth

fighting for anymore?

When did we decide

not to look in our rearview mirrors

and just drive away?

At what point did we realize

we were running

in opposite directions.

When did we decide

there was nothing left of ourselves

to give to one another?

Tell me my love, when did you let go?

#189:

A broken heart will show you

just how strong you really

are capable of being.

It will test your resilience

and even the faith

in a love you no longer have.

It wavers your hope

as it breathes fire

inside your soul.

Burning the good

once lighting up your world.

Yes, a broken heart

is a reflection

of your strength,

but today,

I am

shattered

into a

million pieces.

#190: _____

You want to know

what kind of monster

really lives inside of you?

Swallow a piece of my broken heart.

Let it hide itself deep inside of you.

Allow yourself to feel pain

in places you didn't even

know could hurt.

Close your eyes to shut out the

insane thoughts creating

devilish visuals

at the tip of your mind.

Listen closely as you hear

the suffocating of midnight cries.

You want to know what kind

of monster you really are?

Open wide & taste this broken heart.

#191: _____

Sex between us

was never the same.

No matter how hard I tried

I could still taste her

on your lips,

& smell her on my favorite

part of your neck.

Her scent, though painful

to inhale was ingrained

in the soft tissues

of my nostrils every time

I would exhale.

Every night, I could feel her

in middle of us

as we shared dreams

of our once bright future.

#192: _____

I made the decision

because one of us had to.

One of us had

to be strong enough

to admit this love was reckless,

& toxic,

& damaging,

and no longer what it used to be.

One of us had

to stare denial in the face

because the truth needed to be freed.

One of us desperately

needed to be brave enough

to say enough is enough.

No matter how heart-wrenching

the end would be,

one of us needed

to be the one to say goodbye.

And I'm sorry it had to be me.

#193:
_____

Our love

deserves a second chance.

Our mistakes

deserve a chance to be forgiven

and buried in a place

we can longer

harm one another with them.

Our truths

deserve a chance to have

the masks removed

and to stand boldly beneath the sun.

Our promises

deserve one more chance

to prove everything,

we said that day was worth

the tears you made me cry.

#194: _____

I danced in your shadows.

Your midnight sun covered

all my insecurities,

preventing you

from seeing the scars,

& dead weight,

and skeletons

past loves had left.

Your shadows provided

shelter for all my frailties,

the moon threatened

to expose to you.

#195: _____

As the tears fell

from her eyes,

he regrettably

collected them in his glass.

Holding the rim to his lips

and swallowing

what tasted like anguish.

Savoring each drop,

each time she begged

for his love,

& his affection,

& his attention.

He sipped the remnants

of her leftover love slowly,

knowing it would be

a long road ahead before

he tasted the sweetness

of her forgiveness again.

#196:

He learned long ago his words,

and disregard for her feelings

are what brought them

to this point of no return.

The painful vulgarities

interlaced in each syllable

he shouted tightened her grip

on the shovel,

she now stood next to.

The constant disrespect

of her love

forced her to dig this hole.

His careless way

of leaving her behind

is all the reason she needed

to push him in,

burying this relationship

and walking away.

#197: _____

Our love was covered

in our mistakes.

Drenched in the lessons

we've learned over the years.

Saturated in forgiveness

because we knew it was

worth standing true in.

I rub my hand over your scars

as you do mine.

The beautiful reminders

of the strength we have

from this love we believed

was worth fighting for.

#198:

I'd had my share of

typical men.

The kind of men that

complained about

the impurities, the flaws,

and the corruption

of women.

I would hear them brag

about this one, and that one,

and oh how she,

her and them

did this and that

to make them feel like bigger men.

I'd listened to plenty of tales

from typical, heartbroken,

hypocritical,

damaged men

who would often forget

about the blood on their hands

from all the hearts

they ripped out of

the once innocent,

pure, flawless women

who now do the same.

#199: _____

Vulnerability is a bitch.
She wraps herself
around me and I fight
to be freed from her grip.
I beg for her to feed me,
but hell's kitchen has closed
and there is nothing left
for me to eat.
I sit at the table
waiting for some
nourishment of any kind
only to find emptiness is all
that is being served.

#200: _____

I sit and stare at my heart

in a glass jar,

you placed high on the shelf

so no one can reach it.

I hear it thumping

against the glass

trying to understand

the space it now occupies.

My hands rub over

the place

where you cut it out

and tried to repair.

A reminder my

heart

will forever beat

for only you.

#201: _____

Monogamy is a pill

people swallow

because

they want to believe love

plays by a certain list of rules.

#202: _____

I want to spend the rest of my life

in love with you.

I want to fill all my days

with my ears

pressed up against your chest,

listening to the pace

your heart beats for me.

I dream of spending my nights

underneath your hands

as you trace your fingers over my body,

while the air you exhale

gives life to my flushed skin.

I want to spend the rest of my time

loving you and seeing that love

through your eyes.

#203: _____

Even in the middle of the night

when the darkness

covers our silhouettes,

our eyes, and all the things

that make up who we are,

& the way you hold me

somehow makes the sun

rise in my eyes.

#204: _____

My heart gave up on you

a long time ago.

It's my mind

that continues to betray me

by keeping

the memory of you alive.

#205: _____

That raw sound you hear

is my heart beating

against the iron clad wall

it is trapped behind.

It pounds hard,

hoping to weaken

the inevitable hold

you have on it.

It is trying to break free.

It is trying to escape

the prison your betrayal

trapped it within,

but you won't let it go.

You won't let us be free.

#206:

It would be so good to see you again.

To hear your voice and smell the scent

you used to wear that once drove me wild.

I would love to feel the embrace

that used to warm the insides of my soul,

and the forbidden place between my thighs.

I would love to live in those nights

filled with orgasm after orgasm.

I remember all these things as the thought

of seeing you again excites me.

Then something reminds me to stay away

and protect my fucking heart.

#207: _____

I could slit my wrists open,

bleed all over the table

and you'd still find a way to say

I haven't given you all of me.

You would still find a way

to say I haven't done

all I can to make you happy,

and even if I gave you

my last breath,

I don't know if I ever will.

#208:

It's easier
to let the devil in
than to keep running,
& hiding,
and fighting with him.
But it's twice as hard
to forgive yourself
once you do.
I realized this every time
I let you touch me.
Every time I
opened my heart,
and let you back in.
Every time I watched
you walk back out
with another piece
of my barely, repaired heart.

#209: _____

Once upon a time

when feelings ran high

we called it making love.

Then life settled between us

and it soon became fucking.

More time passed,

more lies were told,

and just when loyalty had enough

it evolved into something

we did until

we were ready to let go.

#210: _____

I miss you.

A part of me left

the moment you

closed your eyes,

and took your last breath.

A broken piece

that no matter how much

time passes,

can never be repaired.

This was the problem

with goodbyes,

this was the problem

with letting go.

#211: _____

We stood in front of each other,

peeling back the layers we hid

behind over the years.

The scorched remains formed

by the lies,

& heartbreak and betrayal,

we added before

we ever came into this.

We shed the excess skin

protecting us from ourselves.

Masks we had become

so comfortable wearing

we forgot who we really

were beneath it all.

#212: _____

I allowed myself

to become a witness

to vulnerability.

I forgave myself

for allowing them

to hurt me,

for hurting myself.

And in the end,

I forged a testimony

to this beautiful thing

I call love.

#213: _____

My heart is ok by itself,

but honestly, it's

better in your care.

Hold it close and keep it safe,

making sure it never breaks.

Protect it from me,

and even you

when it seems either of us

may be careless with it.

Borrow my heart

and when it seems

you have nothing left to fight for,

fight to keep it beating

so that we can both stay alive.

#214: _____

I sit and stare at all the

"I miss you,"

& "I love you,"

& "I'm sorry,"

and "please forgive me" texts.

My heart reminds me

like before

they are only

trap doors that lead

to more trap doors

of an abandoned heart,

I know leads to you.

#215:

She showed him a piece of herself.

The gloom she hid

from everyone else,

but he was like the others

who swore to rescue

her from her sadness.

He turned his back on her.

Not willing to be the light

she wanted,

the healing she longed for,

and the love

she needed to survive.

#216: _____

I touched you

to remind myself

somewhere,

someplace,

inside someone else,

my love lived,

thrived,

existed,

and it was capable

of breathing

outside of me.

#217: _____

I was my own worst enemy,

& the reason my heart broke

harder each time.

I realized the pattern

I created when I looked back

at the ghosts that haunted me.

The many spirits I consumed

and fought to be free of.

The hearts I held prisoner

next to mine.

They all looked at me as I stared at them.

Those were the moments,

I could see they were replicas of you,

in many forms with different

names and faces all along.

#218: _____

I couldn't blame him

for the heartaches

I came searching for.

He was not at fault

for my bleeding heart

and the many mistakes

it made chasing love.

My foolish heart,

would trust anyone,

it was just so naïve.

The warning signs,

& the red flags,

they always shined

so bright before

I even turned

onto that dark corner,

and walked down

that dangerous street,

but I would keep going.

I would keep walking onto

what I knew was a cliff,

awaiting the crashing

of another one

of my loves gone wrong.

#219: _____

His goodbye carried

the weight of the world.

A weight her heart

no longer had to carry

and her shoulders

needed to bear.

#220: _____

We wanted to heal our love,

so, we stayed.

We stood in this moment,

stitching each other back up,

& covering the scars,

we had created.

Wiping away the tears

our suffering freed.

We wanted to start again,

erasing the past.

Two palettes once full

of an array of colors,

now blank ready

to tell a different story.

#221: _____

He kissed me like

he would never again taste

the sweet nectar

that resided

at the crevice of my lips,

while holding my mouth

hostage in hopes

tomorrow would never come.

It was in those moments,

I would give him my all.

I would give him everything

he came looking for,

yearned to taste,

& desired to have,

hoping it would be enough

to coerce him to stay

a little while longer.

#222: _____

You touched my heart

and it shifted.

From the once desolate place

it hid within, you moved me.

Digging my way back

to the surface

it found the light,

and now

it sits comfortably,

beating next to yours.

#223: _____

All I wanted you to do

was protect me from myself.

Protect me from the harm

I sought out in broken places.

The false sense of trust

I often fell victim to.

I wanted you to protect me

from myself,

from sadness,

from the extremities of love,

when it was you

I needed protection from.

#224: _____

He and I,

me and him,

we were like fire.

Burning,

& cleansing,

& destroying,

& restoring

everything in our path.

He and I,

me and him,

we were the beginning

and the end

all wrapped up in one.

#225: _____

I remember the taste

of sweet love

and it sounded like you.

Its eyes listened to me

as its beautiful

words touched my depth.

I remember the taste

of sweet love

and its fragrance

smelled good on you.

#226: _____

He was addicted

to hurting me

and like any pusher,

I stayed and continued

to feed him the drug

we both depended on.

Delusional junkies,

not strong enough

to run from withdrawals.

Lovestruck addicts,

high off

our own destruction

and inability to flee

this toxic love

that was killing us softly.

#227: _____

Love revives my heart
and I realize this moment
no matter how real it feels,
is temporary.
The track marks aligning
my heart is proof
I will soon give in to
the hangover awaiting
my arrival.
Loving you is a sickness,
but my heart doesn't see it that way.
It wants to believe in this false
sense of hope you & I
know will leave me
strung out chasing
that gut-wrenching high again.

#228:

Silence can be crippling.

The absence of your sound

can be vexing,

infuriating,

unbearable,

giving the insanity

room to roam free.

This is what I told myself

to keep holding on.

This is the illusion

I created to make myself

believe without the chaos,

& the unhappiness,

& the dysfunction,

we would not survive.

Ultimately,

I craved your absence more

than your presence.

Proving how

peaceful life could truly be

when it was time to let go.

#229: _____

He is he because I am me.

I am him and he is me.

The color of his eyes exudes

the softness of my skin.

The forever in his lips

caresses my soul's

desire buried within.

I am sex and he is magic.

Together we create love.

#230: _____

You feel like a distant lover,

yet you are right here

beside me.

I am not myself

when I am with you.

I want to be yours,

but I am afraid

of who I may become.

I am not afraid to love you,

but I am afraid

of being responsible

for that love.

I want to hold you

into forever,

but I fear you won't let me in.

#231: _____

I became comfortable in
my being alone.
It wasn't loneliness,
though sometimes
loneliness
had a way of circling my block.
The solitude,
my solitude,
was about survival.
It was about protection.
My heart needed more
time to heal.
More time to prepare
for the next great love.
Heartbreak had been
the last few chapters
of its story,
and it needed time.
Time to walk through

the dark alleys

of loneliness

to find comfort

and stability in being alone.

#232: _____

I buried my happiness

inside of you.

I tucked it away

in the deepest parts of

you,

saving it for a rainy day.

Then one day it rained,

and I looked for you,

but you and my

happiness

were long gone.

Leaving me here

to battle this

brutal storm alone.

#233: _____

Settled between your arms

and beneath

the coolness of your breath,

love reminds me

this is where I am supposed to be.

#234: _____

Here lies the memory

of when I gave a fuck.

I feel nothing

when I hear your name.

These are the words carved

into your headstone

that sits above the grave

I dug for you

inside my heart.

May you and I, rest in peace

as I throw dirt on our memory.

#235: _____

I let you pull me

into this arrangement.

I handed you my heart

and you created

such beautiful,

heart-wrenching acoustics

with its strings.

I let you pimp out the beat

that made up my soul,

and now I am

searching for ways

to turn the channel

and keep the song,

our song

from playing on repeat

over-and-over in my mind.

#236:

I crave the rain

to wash away

his fingerprints,

his kisses,

the taste my lips

refuse to free

and any traces of him

that may be hidden

upon my skin.

#237: _____

I knew it was no longer love

when September

seductively crept in

as the crisp, fall air

reminded me you

wouldn't be coming home.

I had to except this love

was fading like the seasons

as small reminders

like trick or treaters,

and pumpkin spice drinkers,

and cinnamon scented candles

burned in the windows

as November

found its way back to our door

before you did.

I knew for sure by December

this love was no more,

when I couldn't

feel you tucked in my bones

like the aching

I would always feel

from a cold, winter day.

#238:

I was a girl

who tried to save

the wolf,

and he bit me.

I tried to guide him

to a safe place

he could love again,

and he found

something better.

Reminding me

fairy tales

only existed in the corners

of my mind

and everyone

isn't meant to be saved.

#239: _____

Freedom

from my

sleepless nights

came at a price.

So, I sold

the sandman

my memories of you.

#240: _____

I loved you broken

and that was good enough

for you.

Your intentions,

the real ones

you failed to let me see,

never intended

to love all of me,

to let me love all of you.

And I guess in the end

this made us

perfect for one another.

#241: _____

He wanted me to show him

the dark places

where all my demons hid.

I warned him my soul

was a graveyard compiled

of broken promises,

and abandoned loves

from a time, long forgotten.

I opened myself up

to show him

my heart was a hidden closet

with vintage skeletons

hanging delicately

from the hangers.

I lifted the curtains on my soul

for him to could see

it was a haunted place

consumed by ghosts

I fought hard to free.

Shadress Denise

He didn't care,

he didn't run,

he didn't make me feel ashamed.

He reached inside of me

turned on the light,

and told them all

it's time to fucking leave.

#242: _____

You tasted like purple honey.

An empowering,

exotic, overwhelming,

yet authentic flavor

only known to be you.

I wanted to savor you.

I wanted you to lie upon

my tongue

as the walls of my mouth

enjoyed the fullness

of who you were.

The raw, yet rare aroma

that consumed,

and captured, and embodied

my senses,

excited my entire being.

You tasted like purple honey

and now nothing,

and no one else

will ever taste this sweet.

#243: _____

You love me

when I am a beautiful mess

so, I dressed them up for you.

I made them pretty

since seeing them

is what you love most.

I adorned them in

lace and silk.

I wrapped them around

my body

as the rare pearls

hanging from my neck

strangle me.

I embellished them all

in the glitz, and glamour

you made them out to be.

Now my love,

tell me I'm pretty

and I wear your scars well.

#244: _____

I once shouted

I wanted an unbreakable love.

A love that was bulletproof,

and would last until the end of time.

But ha! the joke was on me.

I had no idea what I was asking for.

I had no idea you weren't capable

of giving me that kind of love.

I had no idea how

the wrong kind of love

tested you,

broke you & ruined you.

I was naïve to how it

abandoned you,

left you sitting,

trembling in a dark corner,

staring at the walls

while you held yourself tight.

I was clueless

to its rippling withdrawals.

The screaming at the voices

in my head,

the constant begging them

to release me

from the earth-shattering sound

my heart made against my chest.

It is a horrible feeling

to wrap my heart

in barbed wire because

it was the only way

I could stop it from breaking.

It's even stranger to silence

the curious souls who think

love is the greatest thing to ever find.

But I know better now,

and they won't get me again.

When they ask me

what happened to my heart,

when they ask me why

it no longer wants love,

I will tell them

to protect myself

because I wasn't, it wasn't

brave enough

to survive it, to survive you,

and love lived to die another day.

#245: _____

I left the memory of us on the floor

next to your favorite spot so

you could see it as you walk passed

the place where we

used to hold each other at night.

I left it there because I had no room

to pack it with the things

I was moving on with.

The things I needed

to help me forget about this,

about us.

Of all the memories,

I left the memory of us on the floor,

next to your favorite spot so

when you were ready

you could place it in the closet,

deep in the back

behind the other skeletons,

you decided to hide.

#246: _____

He promised me his love

would never destroy me.

He swore the fire

burning between us

would only be from the passion

we both shared.

He insisted his love

would never leave scars.

In a better world,

it all would have been true.

In a perfect world,

he would be standing here.

In an ideal world,

he would be saving me

from everything going up in flames,

as I try not to suffocate

on the smoke

and ashes our love has become

and now falls at my feet.

#247: _____

How is it we are not meant to be

when part of my soul

sits behind your rib cage,

and my heart is tucked in the

palm of your hand?

When thoughts of me

are engrained

in your mind and the words,

 you speak to me

are laced with love—

how are we not one in the same?

When we bury ourselves

in the erotic tones

of our passionate rhythm,

how can we be anything other

than the property of one another—

how?

#248: _____

He blows on me

and I scatter into a

million pieces across the wind.

I am flying

as the breeze, carelessly

carries me away.

I am a dandelion drifting

throughout the sky—

this is love,

this what love should be.

#249: _____

I wish I could clone the parts

of you that made me smile.

The good intentions

you swore to always have.

The love that left long before you did.

#250: _____

It's funny how two people

can coexist in an empty feeling,

but never find the courage

to leave, or fight for some part

of who they used to be.

I always found it peculiar

how easy it is to normalize

dysfunction,

masquerading it as love.

I gaze from a window

to see the outline of who

we had become

plastered everywhere.

Decorations carved upon

a sidewalk,

as proof love once lived here.

Though the silhouette of disdain

became a smoke screen,

I could still see some

traces of us left behind.

Permanently confined to a place

we dream of being freed from.

Disruptive street art on display

for all the lost lovers to see.

#251: _____

I don't know if he's waiting

for me to save him,

but I can't.

I'm not sure if he's waiting

for me to pray to my God

because he's ashamed to face his,

but it doesn't work like that.

I have nothing to do

with the lies he tells her.

My God won't listen to

my pleas for the pain

he inflicts or the secrets

he keeps hidden

between them at night.

Those burdens, those lies,

those momentary lapses

in judgment & pleasure

are not mine to bear.

I have my own sins

to repent for.

He can keep his own.

#252: _____

I got lost in his eyes.

Lost in the ways

his gaze transcended me

to another place.

In search of who he was

I became a wanderer,

searching through layers

of madness

only find the beauty of

who he really was.

I got lost in his eyes

and when I found my way back,

I didn't return the same.

#253: _____

My heart is full gunpowder

just awaiting the day,

you strike a match

and light it on fire again.

Just be careful you don't burn me

like all the ones before you.

#254: _____

I wanted to be it all for him.

His reason to stay

and want to be here with me.

I wanted to be his choice and the

decision he made for his future.

I wanted him to love me more

then I obviously loved myself.

I wanted all the right things

with the wrong person.

I wanted real love in a lost,

misguided lover.

#255: _____

It wasn't enough for you

to break my heart and destroy

my faith in love.

No, you had to stay,

pull up a chair and be sure

I completely fell apart.

You had to be sure when you

walked out on me for good,

I would be a complete, fucking tragedy

and in no condition to love anyone

else for quite some time.

#256: _____

I started loving myself,

caring for myself,

treating myself better,

the moment I discovered

I was no longer at the mercy

of you loving me.

#257: _____

Misery always cuts the deepest

when the one you love is

inflicting it upon you.

I fell out of his love hard,

collapsing into countless,

unrecognizable pieces.

Fragments of my torn heart

were barely hanging on

while the rest of me

scattered someplace else.

Then I found him,

and he was there

ready to love me

and fix me,

and replace everything

you decided to leave with.

#258: _____

You are more than

the innocence that was taken from you.

More than the blood stains nestled

between the fibers of your sheets,

or the smell of sweat

that won't wash off your skin.

Your silenced voice is stronger

than the loud grunts,

echoing in your ears.

Your life is more than the nightmares

you see with your eyes open,

or shadows that haunt you at night.

One day, you will be more than the dreams

you have closed your eyes to,

or the laughter that has been stolen,

cursing you with eternal tears.

My sweet darling, I know

the rose-colored glasses you once wore

have been removed,

but one day when you are ready,

the sun will kiss your skin again,

and your life won't always be the trauma

that has been your story.

#259: _____

Note after note,

falsetto at the highest octaves,

I could sing loudly for him.

I could find a song

buried deep behind my ribs,

sunken beneath my diaphragm,

& etched in the layers of my lungs

to belt out at his command.

I could sing forever for him

as he composes

beautiful songs

on the inside of my walls.

Key strokes

that cause my orgasms

to become

an orchestra against his ears.

#260: _____

I wonder if he ever reads what I write.

Does he lose himself between the lines,

trying to find redemption for what

he thought was right?

As the words settle within his core,

does he hear the pleading sounds

my heart makes for him,

as he recites them aloud?

Does he ever escape

the haunted memories of us

contained by the blurred lines

in black and white,

or does he find solace in knowing

his transgressions are hidden behind

the imagination

of a girl he no longer loves.

Periodically,

I wonder if he ever reads

what I write and if so,

does he comfort himself

with the same lies he once told me.

#261: _____

Occasionally I find myself

caught between realms of nostalgia.

I daydream about your smell,

your breath on my skin,

and even the way your fingers feel

as they dig deep

into the middle of my thighs.

Most times, I fall prey to

the fantasies of you and I

wrapped up in each other's grasp

as the moans we exhale are

splattered against the walls.

Then there are the times,

when you captivate me

I become paralyzed

and completely submerge myself

in the depth of our desires

as time passes me by.

#262: _____

As I leave, I carry with me

the last kiss you placed upon my lips.

It's softness and lingering after effects

will get me through my darkest moments.

The lust infused nights

we both became drunk off will always

be cradled in the magical crevices of my core.

I'll carry with me, all the

I miss you's,

The soft words that lay gently

on my earlobe when you

would whisper sweet things to me.

I leave with your smile.

How the stretch of it forms across

your face when the light behind

your eyes beam with love.

I'll always carry with me,

all the things I have stored up

that made me fall in love with you.

#263: _____

If we're going to give up

on our love,

let us do it with the same

intense passion

we began with.

If tonight,

like all the nights before

we pretended to be

something we are not,

let us dress up as

Romeo and Juliet,

and let our love die

the greatest love story ever told.

#264: _____

You perfected walking out.

Your footsteps, as they crept

into the distance,

always sounded like

an echo fading away.

The sound of the door as it

closed reminded me

of the last crescendo,

in the dreadful love song

I can finally take off repeat.

#265: _____

I latched onto a star

hoping I could surf the night and ride the waves of

darkness.

I grab ahold of it

hoping I could finally

find my way back to you.

#266: _____

This empty porch that houses

the old rocking chairs

we love to sit in

and the wicker bench

we once made love on,

doesn't seem so empty anymore.

Our disappointments occupy it

as they suffocate the lies,

while our indiscretions

are painted across the walls.

Our once solid foundation,

no longer seems as stable as before.

As the screeching of the

rocking chairs fade into the wind,

I feel the weight

of what we once were

fill up this tiny space that houses

the old rocking chairs we loved

to sit in and the wicker bench

we once made love on.

#267: _____

You should never have

to choose

between loving the person,

you love

and the person

you are in love with.

But here I am,

caught between

deciding to love you

and loving myself.

#268:

I want you to go,

but I want you to stay.

I'm always fighting my heart

over the here and there.

I want you here next to me,

but there is where I know

you can't hurt me.

Distance only prolongs the heartache I know you

standing next to me will cause.

So, here is where you lay

beside me

and I allow this moment

to unravel as it shall.

#269: _____

I never needed you,

that much I knew.

I only wanted my heart to remain

in this game of charades,

we loved to play.

The guessing game,

where we pretended

you were saying one thing

and I convinced my heart

it was something else.

#270: _____

I beg this one thing of you.

Fuck me as hard as you cut into me

with the harsh words, you say.

Give me your pleasurable pain.

#271: _____

There is nothing worse than a half ass lover.
I want someone who will kiss the softest parts of me
when I am in pain while being the mad lover
who will grab me by the neck and forcefully thrust into
me.
I need a lover who will completely throw himself
at the mercy of this love as I have.

Selfishly and unselfishly willing to give into love's will
as his knees bend to engulf the spot that makes us both
weak.
I want a lover who will hold me throughout the night
and when the morning comes, the aroma of coffee
frees us from the intoxicating passion we submerged
ourselves in.

I want lover who will never hesitate
to light my soul on fire when my flame begins to dim.

#272: _____

My heart mimicked

the rest of my body since there

was nothing left for it to fight for.

Too many encounters with

your betrayal

and it grew cold and numb

to your touch,

and even the sight of you.

#273: _____

Step away from my soul.
Climb out of my heart,
and leave with nothing
you didn't come with.

#274: _____

The stars' have depleted themselves

this one time for us.

They are giving us this one night

to shine brighter

than the darkness

that is buried inside of us.

One night,

to light up each other's worlds

the way we use to

and find our way back home.

#275: _____

You traced the outline

of my spine and it reminded me

it was still there,

and all I needed to do

was find the courage to

stand up straight

and walk away.

#276:

I'd come to the realization,

there was nothing left

for you to hurt.

No more bones for you to crush.

No more of my soul

for you to hide your

darkness within.

Not an ounce of my distressed heart

left for you to pull a part.

I could see you were long gone.

Far from places you once lived in,

places you once called home.

#277: _____

You always knew how to move me.

The gravitational pull you have

on my heart calls

for effortless surrender

I relinquish to you.

The freedom I find in you

leaves me always searching

for the core of your complexity.

Your soul's magnetic attraction

connects me to realms

of the love, you easily give.

You are a world of your own

and every day I wake up ready

to discover more of you.

#278: _____

Our lives are an exposé

of unhealthy habits.

Our dysfunction is on display

for all the weary, and broken-hearted

to see and admire.

You smoke.

I drink.

We fuck.

We fight.

And somehow, we convince

ourselves this is all we need

to hold on just a little longer.

These emotional suppressants

are all we need to stop the bleeding

and plug the holes

we continuously fall into.

#279: _____

I don't believe in you
anymore.
I don't believe in us
anymore.
Somewhere,
suppressed deep in
the back of my mind
I held out hope for us,
for this,
but you always had
a way of showing me
it wasn't
worth fighting for.

#280: _____

Don't give me a portion of your love.

Either give me everything

or nothing at all.

I have no more room for rations.

No more room for servings

of anything

that leaves me unfulfilled.

I have grown weak

because of emptiness

and half ass love.

So, either you give me everything

or nothing at all.

#281: _____

I'll always wonder,
When he holds me at night, whose hips
your arms are wrapped around.
When he kisses me, whose body
are your kisses leaving imprints on.

I'll always be curious,
When he makes me laugh, whose lips
you have formed a smile upon.
When he takes me in the shower,
what forbidden places are you making
love in.

I'll always imagine,
When he runs his fingers across my skin,
whose body now lays beneath your warmth.
When a moan escapes my lips,
who screams from the pleasure you are giving.

I'll think about all these things
as I whisper *I love you* to him,
but I'll always wonder where you are

and if we were ever meant to be.

#282: _____

Maybe one day you'll appreciate me.
When you can no longer feel the heat
from my breath on your skin,
maybe you'll appreciate my kisses.

When sound has disappeared
and my heartbeat
no longer occupies this space,
you'll appreciate me.

When the air from a cool night
blows over the empty spot
I used to sleep in,
you'll appreciate
my warm embrace.

When that day comes
and she's nothing of what you
thought she would be,

you'll realize how

you didn't appreciate me.

#283:

I'm staring at your picture

and I want to call you.

I want to tell you that I've been

doing fine since you left.

I want to tell you everything's

been going great.

For some bazaar reason,

I really want to call you,

and tell you I'm over you,

I'm over us, & I've moved on,

but I can't because I'm all alone.

And though I tell myself I'm fine,

I am one drunken night away

from a one-night stand,

& two love songs away

from crying my eyes out,

& three, just three nights away

from taking the pill to help me

forget about you so I can sleep.

Shadress Denise

But I think about you all the time.

When I'm high, and even when I fall

low enough to almost call you.

I no longer scribble your name

in my notebook, or give names

to the future children, yes, I said it,

the future children we will never have,

but your picture, damn that picture

sets me back every time.

Fortunately, you can't see

everything is not great,

and I'm not doing just fine,

but I still want to call you

and to tell you I am

because you don't know

that it would be a lie.

#284: _____

Let me love you one more time.

Let me lie next to you

and hold this moment hostage.

Let me have a piece of forever

as this night

slowly passes us by,

never to return.

Let us lay beneath the stars

as they capture

darkness and shine

their light on our faces.

Hold my hand

as we upstage time

and allow our love to fly free.

Kiss me until

the layers of our lips

can no longer contain

our passion.

Fuck me with the tenacity

of a lover

I may never see again.

Baby, just come with me

and let me love you

one more time.

Hailing from St. Louis, MO, Shadress Denise is an author, graphic designer, and journalist. Her passion for writing began at early age when she fell in love with books. She has been writing poetry and short stories for 15 years. She has currently self-published seven books under her publishing company Blue Indigo Publishing Disturbia, hello. goodbye. never again, Liberated, and Late-Night Thoughts; all poetry books and three novels; Who Do You Love, Who Do You Love Too, and Who Do You Love Now. In 2017, Shadress joined forces with two other St. Louis Authors to release the erotic thriller, Smitten Kitten.

Shadress has earned her BS in Graphic Design and a MA in Communications. During the day, she is an Editor-in-Chief for DELUX Magazine. Shadress continues to build her brand through graphic design as well as writing. Releasing an art line called, Love with a Twist, she combined her love for art & words on greeting cards, postcards, and coasters. Currently residing in her hometown, she is currently preparing to release a variety of upcoming projects.

Be sure to follow her on social media or on her website for book releases and more!

Instagram: www.instagram.com/shadressdenise

Facebook: www.facebook.com/authorshadressdenise

Twitter: www.twitter.com/iShadressDenise.com

Website: https://iamshadressdenise.com

www.ingramcontent.com/pod-product-compliance
Lightning Source LLC
LaVergne TN
LVHW051252080426
835509LV00020B/2935